Blood Splashed Pages

poems of love and illness

Julia Drury Mueller

BookLeaf Publishing

India | USA | UK

Made with ❤ on the BookLeaf Publishing Platform
www.bookleafpub.in
www.bookleafpub.com

Dedication

To family, friends, and doctors who have loved and believed me - you'll find traces of yourselves in these pages.

Preface

The poems I write are blood: I can't stop them but I
would do well to collect them.
april 30

I didn't sit down to a blank page and think of what I'd
say in a book of poems about endometriosis. This
collection is several years' moments of such enamoration
or devastation that the words formed themselves and I
wrote them and watched their rivulets slide down the
pages before I could forget them. I don't so much choose
them as tell you what they are, and I'll blame that if
they're bad. I have others that didn't fit into this book,
thematically or otherwise.

Acknowledgements

Thank you to English teachers who stoke fires in notebooks, the people closest to me who hold the privilege of reading what I write delicately, and BookLeaf Publishing for the push. Thank you to Maggie Bowyer whose writing was formative for forging these words into a book, and to Ada Limón, because as I write I'm stumbling toward whatever she is.

blood splashed pages

you told me I could get paid for my poetry
my darling, I could never sell you

I can't afford the vulnerability, for one,
your blood splashed across the pages for others

and the wine of you, bittersweet on my tongue,
is a sacrament, never a commodity

I would turn the tables of the moneychangers,
cover your face and return you home safe

your beauty isn't for shelves,
but for my palms

world ablaze

Every october the world sets itself ablaze,
one final bid from the trees and mums,
"remember me fondly."

Perhaps we should let corn and wheat die with dignity;
instead we send children giggling into mazes with cider
and tie up the chaff at our doors.

Leaves on apple trees die in childbirth of their fruit
so we may tug them from branches, florid red and sweet,
and color our kitchen with lavish bowls of them
so guests say "they look so beautiful!"
as their bare trees repose uncongratulated.

The ground will decorate itself in a crown of fire
and we'll revel and paint canvases of the splendor
as the grass suffocates under its blanket and dies quietly.

Do they believe they owe beauty, even in death?

My mother found it strange when people would say
"they look so beautiful!"
as bodies, eerily unfamiliar, harden and cool.

But when my grandmother died,
and she lay in her coffin, embalmed and decorated,
my mother said "but she does, she really looks beautiful."

And she did.
She looked younger than I'd ever seen her,
younger than the woman who had collapsed in her
bedroom that week.

Perhaps to fall is to die beautifully.

Perhaps womanhood, even for Mother Earth, is to
decorate yourself when you trouble others,
to accourtre yourself in your most beautiful face when
you get your final affairs in order,

Perhaps I'll unknowingly
dutifully
tragically
put on my mascara on my last morning alive.

dandelion fuzz

Wyn, who will be four on Saturday, is in the far seat,
counting tirelessly.
He's at 27 so far.

Georgie, "two in June," I tell people,
is in the seat near me, yelling everything he knows.
Car, go! Stick! Dandelions!
which is a new word that he's refined to "Diane."

All our clothes are covered in the fuzz of the Dianes.
I say nothing until Georgie prompts me,
saving my breath for the labor of pushing this heavy
stroller.

We all have a role in this ecosystem.
We forget to appreciate each other,
how much each of us lends to this dynamic.

I love going to the farmers market with them.

pointless, greedy beast

There's something insidious about a condition
characterized not by nausea, not by dizziness,
not by the bleeding or bloating, not by fatigue,
but by pain.

Endometriosis is pain.
It's marked by pain,
it's made of pain.

Other symptoms guide toward a diagnosis,
but the diagnosis is an undiluted brew of pain,
the body's indicator of more serious issues,
in this case a conclusion.

The point of this condition is to feel pain.
Its purpose, its ambition, is to unrelent
until you weep and writhe,
to insist
until you beg God for mercy
and wait to find out whether he's merciful.

That is its name, and
it will smile venomously at your familiar face
if you've learned its name.

For 14 years I've had pain attached to my organs.
"It lives where I live."
For incomprehensible hours over those 14 years,
I've cried out to God begging for relief,
for his hand to soothe me, God!
and if he's helped he's been very coy about it.

Too many times
too long to make sense of it,
my body has been lit on fire,
pain beyond comprehension,
sensation beyond what I would have believed
a human could experience without
being killed instantly by sheer force.
There are times I feel certain
only crying out with my voice,
wringing my hands until my nails pierce my skin,
will release the inescapable,
incurable
fire
in my body,
and that has always fallen short.

Yet more often,
far more often,
cumulative months of a quadranscentennial life,

there is instead a low-humming discomfort
that keeps me in bed
no matter how desperately I want to see other humans,
that keeps me nauseated
no matter how nagging my hunger is,
that feels like tangled pillow hair
and second-guessing my sanity
and more time on my phone than I ever want again.

It smells like ketorolac tromethamine,
it feels like isolation.

I wish it only felt like isolation,
that it didn't have monstrous,
malicious hands wringing my organs,
and a jack prying at my hips
until I rip down the middle.

But it does.

And I will burn the skin across my abdomen for days
even if it adds to the pain,
because it's a pitiful kind of relief,
the way a leech relieves a virus.

8:01AM

That's love,

I smell your sweat and still pull myself closer
because as I lie next to you in the quiet
our want of each other is eager
and your messy hair and your humanness
cannot dampen your gravitational pull

You apologize for your morning breath
but a star is the most wonderful thing
to the body that pirouettes ever around to feel its
warmth

Make me sweat too
I don't care
Keep me close

heartbreak

in a folding chair in an auditorium
I watched a friend's friend sing his poetry,
and maybe it's because his dulcet tones
stirred something in me,

but when I saw the woman in front of me
rest her head on the shoulder of a friend
I felt my heart burst inside of me

and as the warm blood dripped
from the backs of my ribs,

I committed the sight to memory
so I could paint it later.
I knew I could lower my expectations
                lower
           lower
and still the painting wouldn't capture what I hoped,

and it would live in a notebook that only I would open
and it would die with me,
but it was so warm, I had to try

from my first night on my own

What was once a name on my lips,
an idea to be congratulated,
a fantasy to be indulged,
is now realized.
It burst forth out of conversation
into an explosive flurry of experience.
That faraway land, that elusive, fantastic Chicago -
it now sprawls out all around me,
fraught with scents and sounds,
intricate in design,
from rats to record stores.
This long-held dream and hard-pursued ambition
has manifested itself in
the dusty white walls and old carpet
that envelope me eight stories up.

mother faithful

tireless
tireless
tireless

my mother is faithful tirelessly

the sun wheels around the sky and I grow and wrinkle
and my mother reads new books and new books and
new books about the faith

she pray prayers she never has, somehow

she has more to learn
my lifetime long, she's wanted to learn more
how does she still have room for more?

Lord that I inherit her appetite
I've never hungered for anything like my mother
hungers for decades of more

moving

This home was nothing,
then everything we owned burst into it all in one day
and it was home
and it became warm.

For two years I opened the door
hung up my keys
and he was sitting on the couch,
happy to see me.
Our feet know these floors.

I painted the wall my favorite color
and in return,
the faucet gave me warm water
for fragrant baths.

I bled here.
We held each other and cried into the night here.
I learned new ways to be mad at him
standing at the kitchen sink.

We kissed in every room.
Sometimes the walls were filled
with the ringing laughter of all our friends,

and more often it was silent,
flooded with quiet, unappreciated light
from the big windows
and unnoticed warmth from the radiators.

I put pumpkins on the table
and hung paper snowflakes from the ceiling
and filled vases with cut flowers
and grew my plants in the windowsill.

The window opened for me
so I could hear the cars and dogs
and breathe the fresh air
and go on living.

We scuffed the walls and
washed the windows and
God, how could anything pull me away from this place?

But now it's time to roll up the rug again
and hand the key to a man in an office
after it's lived 2 years in my pocket.

I hope the next people fill this place
with love like we did.
I hope we fill the next place
with love like we did this place.

I wonder if a hermit crab cares
when it's outgrown its shell,
or if a butterfly remembers fondly
the walls of its chrysalis.
These walls heard me sing
and held framed photos of people I love,
so I'll remember them fondly.

Forward my mail to West Grand, please.

from a spare bedroom during a party

Endometriosis, what a medical word,
and it means loneliness.
It's dinner in a private room,
everyone's muffled laughter through the walls.
It's laying in bed in my best makeup and pretty hair.
I had big exciting plans before the pain ruptured me.
I knew it would start today between 3 and 6,
because it had to
because it can't just be physical pain,
it has to isolate and embarrass and change plans.
And I, in this spare room,
brood and bleed,
ache and weep.
I wish it were okay to socialize in pain.
Wheel me down to the party on a stretcher,
forgive me if I grimace,
but talk to me,
make me laugh,
mill around near me,
let me watch you play games together.
Everyone needs people,
and I wonder how different disabled lives could be.
Do you mind if I wince?

I get to be a woman, too

I am beautiful and so are the things I create
The tulips and carnations I arrange
and the euphonious laughter of people who love me
I know there is good because I watch it pour out of me
25-year-old women are beautiful and I have become one

for Vivian, who's 1

all, all, ALL the time!

I think about your shoes and I think about your hair,
I think about you here and I think about you there.
I think about your mind and all the things you know,
I think about how fast you run and where you like to go.
I think about your laugh and I think about your smile,
I think about your love and I think I like your style!
I think about your books sitting neatly in a pile,
I think about you and it makes everything worthwhile.
I think about Larry Boy and your Teddy and Pooh,
and guess what. I think about Edmund too!
I think about you, and someone else, guess who!
I think about Mama and Daddy, and I think of you anew!

a shipment of painkillers spoiled in the mailroom

I had to fight against my body,
or not my body,
but the pointless, indifferent disease racking it,
with acetaminophen, naproxen sodium, and a heat pad.
Most people don't know how much pain you can feel.
I tried to see past the pain in my mind's eye
to anything in the apartment that would turn it off,
all sensation, please, sedation, death, anything!
I couldn't think beyond survival of the next second
of pain that felt like it needed to be exorcised.
I opened my jaw to its widest,
like unhinging it snakelike would let the horror out.
Will Byers in a shed, the monster burned from him.
When people ask and I think they can handle honesty,
I tell them it's being burned alive,
not strictly a searing sensation, but an urgency,
fire lapping at your skin, melting flesh, burning bones,
but this never burns you up, never finishes you off,
never starves for fuel.
An ER doctor told me *"most women go through this."*
One who does wrote that this disease
is true body horror, and she wouldn't wish it on anyone;
that's what I say, if you can handle honesty.

Directors have tried to portray the most horrific,
most disturbing things that can happen to a body,
because people will pay to be intrigued and squirm,
but the excruciation I've met is horrific
beyond anything a movie could portray.
My coach once told me it's no excuse to miss practice.
The sounds I heard from myself that night
and the expressions I felt on my face
were new to me, and they terrified me.
The veil of my medications was pulled back
and I saw the insanity of raw pain that lurks behind it.
A man close to me once suggested Lamaze breathing.
But breathing on a fire fans the flames;
poor advice for an effigiated woman.

I think you're mean

A decade ago
The idea that I could shred my skin
and tear out my organs
and I would finally find rest
from being a disappointment to others
Cozied itself in my spinal cord
and I have not lived without it since

A sensitive person makes others walk on eggshells
I'm sympathetic to that
I've paid my dues to it for years
and if I could find a way to be different I would
God knows I've spent thousands of dollars
asking professionals to make me different

And they haven't

All they've taught me is that it's okay
to be soft and to ponder what I'm owed
And the first thing I'm owed is from me to me,
a commitment to the boundaries
against things people say and do and show to me
that make me want to destroy myself

I can't be who you're asking for
and I know you're frustrated
and it makes me want to fill my lungs with the lake
so they never have to be disappointed again
in the body they will not find

fruit for my love

Tonight I sat next to a three-year-old
two trays of Crayola watercolors
and he smudged on his paper and
said his blotches were for Mama

I, as always when presented with paint,
reflexively created fruit,
dotting seeds onto strawberries, and I knew
tomorrow is Valentine's Day

and I would give this page of fruits
to my husband and I'd pose
and say I made him a Valentine's Day card,
knowing he'll crack open wide and laugh smittenly

and accept because the personality
of someone who works with kids is with me
long after I leave work
and he loves me for it.

My five-year-old draws rocket ships
and they're always for Mama
Never in that woman's life did she care
about aerospace engineering,

but the boy she made drew this one for her.
Children do this,

they recreate the things they love most
in all the world and offer them to us,
they clumsily throw love toward us
in any way they can imagine,

and we soak it up because we know,
we understand.

this is how the years pass

Washing my windows,
thinking "so this is how the years pass."

We sleep together in the same bed every night,
and every few years the bed changes.

The pictures in my camera roll
go from being last week to 4 years ago.

"So this is how the years pass."

I'm wiping grime from the windows
that will return in a few weeks
and then I'll wipe them again.

The tulips in my kitchen are opening,
I'm listening to a record I bought a few months ago,
I'm cleaning my home,
our lives are changing,
and it just feels like breathing.

sense of home

I pretend to be a lot of things for a lot of people, so there's a rare sense of home and purpose when I get to talk about something that's truly me. And in autumn it's pumpkins. When I was small I would go out to the garden to turn the pumpkins so they wouldn't have flat spots, careful of the stems and undersides of the leaves, sharp on little hands and uncalloused skin. I remember the way we could drop one pumpkin seed in soil and we'd have vines sprawling out of the spot for years, or so it seemed to me. Pumpkins are funny that way. Now I live in the city and my feet walk on concrete everywhere I go, but when I see an ad for a pumpkin festival in the city or I see them in front of a grocery store, vibrant orange and arranged by size, it takes me back to those years when the most exciting thing was the way our pumpkins would just keep growing and growing and growing and we would hope with all our little might that we would have the biggest ones in the county, and Dad would exhibit them proudly by decorating the church stage with them. That's me. I'll take interest in new things because it's good and I love the people who are interested in them, but I'm a kid growing pumpkins for the church stage.

winter meditation 1

Do you think when summer comes we'll be happy?

I want to ask my friends this,
constantly,
bloodletting it for genuine curiosity,
but it would just worry them;
they'd clean the wound rather than answer

I looked in the mirror today
and I saw someone so pale and so sad,
like a wilted plant;
organisms need warmth and light to live,
and I need to reconcile
what I want with what I can have

But,
the Sun is in my kitchen,
reheated vegan chili warm in my hands,
a band I used to like dancing to in the vents

Summer is so far, but the Sun has come home
and my veins are warm for now

winter meditation 2

Repeat after me:
I am allowed to go to the grocery store
when it's dark out.
My day does not end when the sun sets.
I may light my own sky
with the fiery radiance of rebellion.
I may create new worlds in the dark
with my needle and thread
pages and wax
fresh ingredients and simmering oil
hands and my lover's skin
violin strings and honeyed tones
yoga mat and living room floor
books and *conjugaisons nouvelles*
serums and balms and pigments
cutest clothes and highest heels
and loudest laugh, shivering under my warmest coat.
I will not hibernate.
I will live a second life the sun doesn't know about,
richly fulfilling,
metamorphosing me into someone
the spring sun won't expect.

how sinister,

how demented and damned,
that my pain isn't just for me,
it hurts everyone who loves me,
that my husband knows the sound
of my voice crying out in pain
so well,
that my mama has to hear it,
not only my squeaky voice
when I was small and I scraped my knees,
but my voice as a woman,
late in the night down the hall,
or in the middle of the day
when I was supposed to be somewhere else,
and from outside the bathroom door,
checking on me.
She has to hear the voice of her child
whose body is on fire.

The pain is for me.
I'll feel it and be mad about it
because it's mine,
but it's not meant for them,
it's just too big for my body and finds its way out,
I'm so sorry,

and then my dad,
my best friend,
people I cherish,
have to see the face of a woman they love
with lines across it,
eyes squeezed shut,
teeth gritted,
scratch marks down her cheeks;
have to hear me groaning, shouting,
seeing if God hears my voice
better than he'll hear my thoughts,
wailing in pain.
Hellishly vile.

preening feathers

love me like an animal,

by which I mean watch my back when we're out
and sleep next to me because it's warmer
and eat with me and starve with me

I don't think a proximity bond is a bad thing,
it's romantic in a different way
than shaken feathers and dancing feet
this life is so difficult and
I don't mind that we love
just because we both feel safe here

we've shown care for each other,
now my territory is yours,
and I'll snap my jaws at you sometimes
and then we'll clean each other and be okay

will you always preen my feathers for me?

www.ingramcontent.com/pod-product-compliance
Lightning Source LLC
Chambersburg PA
CBHW071236140726

47996CB00007B/2636